D0056449

# wedding zen

# wedding zen

*Calming Wisdom for the Bride*

*By Susan Elia MacNeal*

*Illustrations by Rachell Sumpter*

**CHRONICLE BOOKS**
SAN FRANCISCO

Library of Congress Cataloging-in-Publication Data available.

ISBN 0-8118-4415-3

Manufactured in China.

Designed by Tracy Sunrize Johnson

The illustrator wishes to thank her parents John and Cheryll
Sumpter, and designers Tracy Johnson and Brett MacFadden
at Chronicle for their creative help and patience.

Distributed in Canada by Raincoast Books
9050 Shaughnessy Street
Vancouver, British Columbia V6P 6E5

10 9 8 7 6 5 4 3 2 1

Chronicle Books LLC
85 Second Street
San Francisco, California 94105

www.chroniclebooks.com

*To my husband, Noel MacNeal,
for his unwavering love and support.*

# table of contents

# 2 Wedding and Wanting

# 3 Making Your Big Wedding Decisions with "Right Effort"

# 6 The Big Day and Beyond

# 7 You Mean There's Life After the Wedding?

# introduction

Congratulations—you're engaged!

Getting married is supposed to be one of the happiest times of your life. So why are you feeling so stressed?

Well, relax. Even the most sane and balanced person can feel a bit, er, challenged while planning a wedding. And it's okay to feel frazzled; in fact, it's perfectly normal. Most people have a moment or two—or five— where they're ready to elope to Las Vegas.

Wedding planning *can* get crazy. There are a lot of expectations, and a lot of pressure. Everything (and everyone) around you is changing. Whether you're trying to lose fifty pounds in five months to zip up a certain dress, fighting the urge to spend too much money, or coping with divorced parents who are bickering over seating arrangements, you may find yourself in some anxiety-provoking situations.

Which is where *Wedding Zen* can help.

Zen is a philosophy for living that's compatible with any religion. It's about being aware, present, and real. It's about living in the now and taking the Middle Way. And it's about practicing nonattachment—making plans, but holding onto them lightly. With a little Zen perspective, you'll be able to relax, free yourself from excessive material and emotional needs, and be more compassionate and honest. You'll plan your wedding with love, kindness, and humor. As a result, your wedding will be a relaxed, genuine, and truly joyous occasion.

Making a lifelong commitment to the person you love, in the midst of family and friends, is something to celebrate. No matter the style, size, or location of your wedding, the most important thing is for you to delight in the feeling in your heart.

After all, *every* day is "the big day," when you really think about it.

chapter *1*

and you

You've no doubt heard the word *Zen* and have an idea of what it means—maybe monks with shaved heads in saffron-colored robes, incense, and little silver bells come to mind. But you've probably never heard Zen mentioned in relation to wedding planning. Well, Wedding Zen is a philosophy of wedding planning, loosely based on the philosophy of Zen Buddhism.

In this chapter, you'll learn some of the basic concepts of Zen and how to apply them as you dive into wedding planning. You'll learn how to live in the present. You'll get to know yourself better. You'll practice nonattachment when things don't go your way. You'll learn to let go of the myth of the "perfect" wedding. And you'll do all this while you're breathing, laughing, walking, keeping a journal, and spending some time alone.

Remember: Zen is now. It helps us stay in the present and relinquish control. (Yes, letting go of the illusion of control will help you feel better. Don't believe it? Read on!)

Anyone can do it. It's easy. You just have to begin.

## The Rule of **Engagement:**

### *Being in the Present Moment*

When you're engaged to be married, there's so much to do. You need to schedule the officiant, order the dress, buy the invitations, and take care of hundreds of other details. It's easy to let the days slip by in a flurry of planning, at a time when each and every one should be savored.

The only real rule of being engaged? Be in the present moment. Being fully present is the cornerstone of Zen; when you're truly aware, you're not fretting about the past or dreaming about the future—you are firmly rooted in the present. (It's as easy and as difficult as that.) One way to stay in the moment is to be aware of your five senses: How does your body feel right now? What do you hear? What do you see around you? Do you smell or taste anything? Perhaps most important: What emotions are you experiencing?

Try focusing your attention on the present often—while waiting in traffic, cooking dinner, talking with your partner. With practice, you'll begin to live a more mindful life. Right now.

**But what minutes! Count them by sensation, and not by calendars, and each moment is a day, and the race a life.**

**—Benjamin Disraeli**

This above all: to thine own self be true,
And it must follow, as night the day,
Thou canst not then be false to any man.

—*William Shakespeare*

## **Who** *Are You?*

### *Zen and the Art of Being Yourself*

Pretend you don't have to please anyone but yourself. "Do I *really* want to get married in a long white dress? Do I actually *need* ten bridesmaids? All in bubble-gum pink taffeta?" We're often encouraged—by parents, friends, even ourselves—to be someone we're not, especially on our wedding day. It can be exhausting. Zen helps us question the assumptions we hold about ourselves, ones that influence our wedding planning.

Take some time to really think about your wedding day. What's important to you? What images come up in your imagination? Make a list of those things. Pretty long, huh? Now go down that list and try to figure out which ones are truly coming from you—and which ones might be coming from outside influences. You might even try the following:

*If I didn't have to please my family, I would*

_____

*If I wasn't worried about what people would think, I would*

_____

*If I only had to please myself, I would*

_____

By learning what you really want for your wedding—as opposed to what other people want or what society dictates—you'll begin the process of getting to know the real you. Should you decide that you do want the white dress and the ten attendants, won't it be good to know that that's what *you* really want? When you take nothing for granted, you gain an interesting perspective on your choices and how you live your life.

If the only prayer you ever say in your entire life
is thank you, it will be enough.

—Meister Eckhardt

## The Myth of **the "Perfect" Wedding**

Sometimes our longing for the "perfect" wedding leads
to frustration (or *dukkha* in Zen-speak). We invest so
much in the idea of "the perfect day" that we imbue it
with the power to give and take away our happiness.

No day can be perfect (although it can be perfectly
wonderful). By trying too hard to make it so, we take all
of the life, joy, and spontaneity out of it, and we don't
appreciate all the moments leading up to it.

Remind yourself to notice the wonderful things that
happen every day (even on the not-so-fantastic days).
Each night, as you're going to sleep, think of at least
five things—from the silly to the sublime—that happened during the day for which you're grateful.

DUKKHA *is the Sanskrit word for the suffering brought on
by our attachments, desires, and wants.*

## Micromanaging and **Meditation**

Even after you successfully let go of the myth of the "perfect" wedding, there are still a thousand wedding details for you to think about. They buzz around in your head, distracting you from the present moment. How can you enjoy your engagement—without being constantly distracted by your to-do list?

Meditation is one way. The act of meditating is at the heart of Zen. *Zazen* (sitting mediation) is perhaps the best-known form. First, choose a sitting position. The lotus position (sitting on the floor with legs crossed and each foot on top of the opposite thigh) is traditional, but hey—it can be difficult for those of us with tight hips. You can also sit cross-legged on the floor, or sit as you would normally in a chair.

Once you're settled, resting your hands comfortably in your lap, close your eyes and simply be present, bringing your attention to your breath. You don't need to change your breathing, but do be aware of it—the coolness of the air as it comes into you, the feeling of expansion in your lungs, the warmth of your exhalation. Sit still, breathing naturally.

It might feel difficult. As the minutes go by, your mind might wander ("Did I turn off the iron? I really need a haircut. . . . What's for dinner tonight?") and your nose might itch. Simply acknowledge the thoughts and feelings that arise—and then let them go, returning to your awareness of your breathing. With practice, meditation will help you experience full awareness of the present.

ZEN *is the Japanese word for meditation.*

ZA *is the Japanese word for sitting.*

ZAZEN *means sitting meditation.*

THE LOTUS POSITION *is a traditional meditation pose meant to suggest the perfection of the lotus flower. It's said to be the position in which Buddha became enlightened.*

## *Planning **without Obsessing***

Zen has everything to do with giving up the illusion of control. Whether you're planning a simple wedding in your own home or a big bash halfway around the world, making wedding plans can make control freaks of even the most centered souls.

The truth is that we're not in control, ultimately. Life goes on, people are unpredictable, and stuff happens. You yourself can decide whether to freak out and obsess—or get on with your wedding plans and your life.

That's not to say you shouldn't make plans, check on details, and follow through. Of course, you're going to make lists, keep folders, and make follow-up phone calls. When that's what you're doing, do it with your utmost concentration. But when you're done, come on back to your regularly scheduled life.

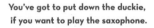

**You've got to put down the duckie,
if you want to play the saxophone.**

**—Sesame Street**

*Famous diarists include Samuel Pepys, Anaïs Nin, May Sarton, James Boswell, Ralph Waldo Emerson, Virginia Woolf, Anne Morrow Lindbergh, Henry David Thoreau, and Marie Bashkirtseff.*

Keeping a **Journal**

*"Dear Buddha, today I . . ."*

Your engagement is a wonderful time for writing in a journal. If you don't keep one already, treat yourself to a beautiful notebook and pen, and take some time to write in it each day. It's a wonderful way to carve out some quiet time and get in touch with your real thoughts and feelings. Having a private space to express yourself honestly, and without judgment, will help you stay aware of what you're really feeling as you plan your wedding; it's also a great keepsake.

Just make sure to keep it in a safe place.

## The Wonder of **Walking**

Sometimes planning your wedding can make you worry. It's easy to lose sight of priorities and feel anxious, jittery, and restless. When sitting still doesn't seem possible, take a walk instead. Walking meditation is called *kinhin* in Japanese; Zen practitioners alternate periods of sitting meditation with periods of walking meditation. Experiment with each to see what works for you.

As with *zazen*, be fully present as you walk. Concentrate on your breathing. Walk mindfully, at a medium pace. When your mind begins to wander, simply acknowledge your thoughts and return to the present.

It's also great practice for walking down the aisle.

## Yoga: *The Moving Meditation*

Many people also head to the gym to slim down and
tone up for their wedding day. Weightlifting and cardio
are great, but have you ever considered trying yoga?

Yoga is a form of "moving meditation." In addition to
helping you be in the moment and focus on your breath,
the poses—or *asanas*—help your flexibility and strength.
(And your triceps will look fabulous!)

While there are some wonderful books and tapes available, it's a good idea to check out a class or two first,
especially if you're a beginner or out of practice. Work
with a teacher who's concerned with proper technique
and alignment; after all, you don't want to limp down
the aisle.

**You wouldn't add white to your laundry
to make it clean—you add detergent.
Asanas are like the detergent that
cleans your mind.**

**—Swami Satchidananda,
related by the artist Peter Max**

## Keeping your **"Zense"** of Humor (Get It?)

One thing about planning a wedding is that it brings you in contact with people—officiants, caterers, musicians, and so on—that you wouldn't necessarily meet otherwise. You'll probably encounter a lot of different people, and you'll need to get a feel for them and their work—not to mention their fees.

Many of these people will be absolutely wonderful. When you meet the odd bird who's not, rely on your sense of humor and laugh at how silly the whole process is. Zen masters value a sense of humor.

Be open to laughing at the wacky nature of the universe. Laughter relieves stress, eases tension, improves circulation—and it's absolutely free.

# Dieting **Dharma**
## (or The Middle "Weigh")

*Oy.* One of the first things most women do when they get engaged is to start a diet. There's that wedding dress to fit into, plus the wedding photos that will haunt you for eternity, not to mention the bikini you might want to wear on the honeymoon.

Of course, we all want to look our best, but there's a different, more Zen way to approach food: mindfulness and moderation. When we're mindful about the food we choose, we don't eat on the run, stuff ourselves with junk, or comfort ourselves with cookies when we've had a bad day. (Well, maybe a few. But not the whole bag.)

The "Middle Way"—moderation in all things—is an important part of Zen philosophy.

THE EIGHTFOLD PATH *is a guideline for living. It's composed of right effort, right understanding, right thought, right speech, right action, right livelihood, right mindfulness, and right concentration.*

DHARMA *is the word for truth realized by the Buddha. Of course, there is no "dieting dharma" per se, but one of the precepts of the Eightfold Path is right action, which includes control of the appetites.*

**THE MIDDLE WAY**

*is the way of moderation, neither opulent nor ascetic.*

chapter *2*

# wedding

## and wanting

It is human to want things; it's absolutely normal. But obsessive craving, as you probably know by now, doesn't lead to happiness.

One of the biggest problems that come with planning a wedding is the *multibillion*-dollar bridal industry. Bridal business is big; to sell products, companies deliberately encourage your insecurities that your wedding won't ever measure up to those shown in their ads.

People feel more centered while planning their wedding if they're free from excessive want, whatever that means to them: status, prestige, an eight-tiered gold-leaf-covered cake, or a Vera Wang dress. Unless we learn to control, and not be controlled by, our desires, we'll never be able to experience real joy.

Becoming mindful of your attachments and demands will ease your "I need this, I deserve this, I *must* have this for my perfect day" tendencies. This chapter gives you some ideas for letting go, whether it be material possessions or the impossible expectations of others.

# Take a Break from *Bridal Magazines*

It's true. You *can* become addicted to bridal magazines. The world portrayed in their thick, glossy pages is always perfect—the bride never has pores (let alone a blemish), the bridesmaids are all size two, and no one ever worries about money.

Even though bridal magazines can be great sources of ideas and resources, it's important to remember that the weddings they show have *nothing to do with reality* (even the so-called real ones). They're also vehicles for advertising. The more longing, envy, and insecurity the ads create in us, the more tempted we are to buy products that will make us and our wedding day "perfect."

It's hard not to be swept away by glorious images of brides and bouquets. But if you feel yourself experiencing *dukkha*, take a minute to remember what's really important.

THE FOUR NOBLE TRUTHS *are at the heart of the Buddha's teachings:*

- *It's human to experience suffering, or dukkha.*
- *Suffering is caused by desire or attachment, at the expense of knowledge of reality.*
- *Suffering can be eliminated when we give up desire.*
- *Desire can be eliminated by following the Eightfold Path.*

## Staying Out of **Wedding Debt**

The average wedding in the United States costs over $24,000—that's about $5,000 per hour.

Money—specifically debt—is one of the major sources of stress for married couples. The Buddha knew that desire led to suffering, but even he couldn't have imagined the wedding loans that some banks offer. Or the havoc compound interest can wreak on your future financial plans, such as buying a car or a house or starting a family.

'Tis the gift to be simple, 'tis the gift to be free,
'Tis the gift to come down where we ought to be.

—*Shaker hymn*

To avoid debt, concentrate on what's *really* important as you plan your wedding: making your vows with your partner, and celebrating with your family and friends. Right? *(Right?)* Your wedding is about your future. Don't mortgage your future for just one day.

## Perusing **Purchases**

To keep from spending too much, learn to control, and not be controlled by, your material desires. Let go of things that don't last, and that ultimately aren't important. You know—the *stuff* part of the wedding.

One way to exercise control over materialist urges (and we all have them) is to give yourself time to really think over the big purchases, and not just buy on impulse. So many wedding decisions are made in the heat of the moment. Take some time to rationally consider what exactly you're buying, why you're buying it, and how much you really want it. Will you still want it two weeks from now? In a month? When you think back on your wedding decades from now, will you even remember it?

Think long and hard before spending and you'll return from your honeymoon free from worry about how you'll pay off the wedding.

## Leggo Your *Ego*

It's the ego that says, "I must have that dress I can't afford or I'll look gauche," "My wedding has to be as big as my sister's," or "My wedding will be ruined if we can't have it at the Ritz."

Sometimes we lose perspective and begin to believe that it's crucial to have a certain dress, florist, maid of honor— or whatever. If we don't get what we want, we create turmoil and anxiety. It's not having a particular dress or flowers that makes us happy or despondent—it's the *meaning* we assign to these things, and our demand for them, that can make us crazy.

By being open to different scenarios, we can regain our sense of balance and perspective.

**Our life is frittered away by detail. . . .
Simplify, simplify.**

**—Henry David Thoreau**

## I Love You *versus I.O.U.*

If you are accepting wedding funds from relatives or friends, consider—how is it affecting your relationships with the givers? Are you feeling pressure to have the wedding that *they* want, as opposed to the one you want? Since they're the ones footing the bill, how much say do they get?

Money can be a touchy subject. When accepting wedding funds, it's important to keep listening to yourself. If there are strings attached, either stated outright or implied, be honest: Is it bothering you? How much?

Although it can be difficult (especially when the subject is money), keep the lines of communication open. Talk to the people who are writing the check about their expectations. Let them know if what they want is making you feel uncomfortable, so that you can work to find an arrangement that everyone can accept.

While life is sometimes about compromise, if you feel you're being false, then it's time to take a step back and consider the arrangement's real cost. You and your partner may decide that it's not in your best interest to use the offered funds. Although you'll have to scale back your plans, it may be worth it to have the wedding you want—and not strain important relationships.

## Rings *and Things*

A ring is a ring is a ring—unless it represents something else. Some people can get attached to the idea of the ring—how big it is, how expensive, which finger to wear it on, and so on. Some people even go to the extreme of wearing fake diamonds, in a misguided attempt to keep up with the proverbial Joneses.

Should you find ring-related *dukkha* happening to you, try approaching the idea of the ring with absolutely no preconceptions. Ask yourself: If left to your own devices, would you want a ring at all? If so, why? Would you want to give your partner a ring? What hand and finger would you wear it on? What kind of ring would it be? And— most important—what would the ring symbolize to you?

# What Do You Care
## *What Other People Think?*

*Dukkha* is also created when we care too much about what other people think. Yes, of course you want people to enjoy themselves at your wedding. But that's different from deconstructing what everyone might think, and basing your choices on that. And even if other people don't agree with your wedding choices—your dress is chartreuse instead of white, the cake is chocolate as opposed to vanilla, the entrée is vegan—so what?

In some ways, a wedding is like dinner theater: you have your leads, supporting characters, costumes, and props. And, as in the theater, you have your critics and their inevitable reviews. But if you try to please everyone, you'll end up pleasing no one, least of all yourself.

**What do you care what other people think?**

**—*Richard Feynman***

chapter 3

making your
    big wedding decisions
    with
"right effort"

As you travel farther along the wedding-planning path, there are big decisions to be made: What style of wedding to have? Who will officiate? Whom to invite? What to wear? What to serve at the reception?

"Controlling my *dukkha* sounds well and good," you may be thinking, "but I'm going to Brunhilde's Bridal Boutique to choose my dress today, and I need more specific advice. How's Zen going to help me with that?"

Well, there aren't any particular "rules" in Zen, but there is the Eightfold Path, a Zen guideline for living with more joy and less *dukkha*. It consists of right understanding, right thought, right speech, right action, right livelihood, right mindfulness, right concentration, and right effort.

Right effort is about being the best version of yourself that you can be—you know, the kind and compassionate self. The self who makes plans but holds onto them lightly.

In this chapter, you'll find advice on choosing your wedding style, wedding dress, location, guest list, rituals, flowers, and photography—all the nuts and bolts of a wedding. The decision-making process can get stressful. But as you go about your planning, consider right effort—and keep breathing.

## Your *Wedding Style*

You undoubtedly want your wedding to be a genuine expression of your and your partner's personalities. So who are you as a couple? Are you traditional, bohemian, outdoorsy, sophisticated—or something completely different? In your journal, jot down ten adjectives that describe you as a couple. Do you see a theme emerge?

Instead of thinking of your wedding and reception as "The Wedding," try thinking of them as an extension of how you celebrate in your so-called regular life. What kind of entertaining do you do? Backyard barbecues, sit-down meals with formal flower arrangements and multiple courses, or get-togethers at the hottest new boîte in town?

What you already gravitate to and what you're comfortable with is a good jumping-off point for your wedding plans.

**Know thyself.**

*—Plutarch*

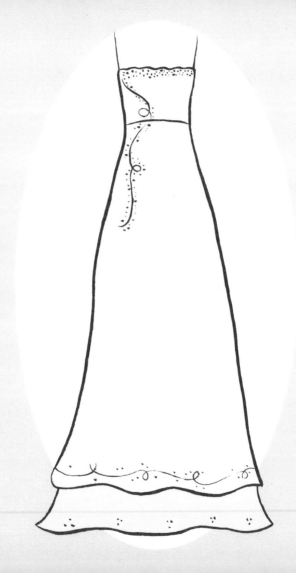

## Sartorial *Satori*

What to wear to your wedding—perhaps no other fashion choice offers such a public display of your style and taste. Will you choose a traditional long white dress, a red and gold sari, a Marlene Dietrich-inspired pantsuit, or something else entirely? And what will that choice mean to you?

Let your imagination run wild. If you only had to please yourself, what would you wear? When you finally get to the point where you can look at yourself in your wedding attire and say, "Yes, it's beautiful—and it's me," you'll have found satori.

SATORI *is the Japanese word for enlightenment.*

**Elegance does not consist in putting on a new dress.**

**—Coco Chanel**

## The *What, Where, and When*

Next to choosing who will officiate and what to wear, the decision about where and when to hold your ceremony and reception is the most expressive of your personal style. Will you marry in a church lit by candlelight—or under pine trees in the morning sun? Try to envision yourself at your wedding. What season is it? What time of day is it? What kind of space do you see?

One way to simplify life for yourself and your guests is to hold the ceremony and reception near each other, or even in the same space. There's something wonderful about keeping the emotion of the day flowing; plus you don't have to worry about guests getting lost or stuck in traffic.

## Nuptials and **Namaste**

Lots of rituals and traditions are associated with Western weddings, such as saying "I do," wearing white, and exchanging rings.

There are many Zen rituals that are compatible with any religious ceremony. One is the practice of bowing, with the hands held together in prayer pose. The bow symbolizes the divine nature in you acknowledging the divine nature in others.

What kind of rituals do you envision at your wedding? Consider some that are meaningful to you and share them with your partner. Would you like to add any of them to your wedding ceremony? Why not create a ritual for your wedding with specific meaning to you?

NAMASTE *is a Sanskrit word meaning "I bow to the divine within you, which is the divine within me."*

## Your *Wedding Party*

There may be a lot of people telling you whom you "should" choose for your wedding party. Your mother thinks you should include your second cousins, your betrothed wants you to include his sister, while you really want to pick your six best friends—two of whom happen to be male.

You need to please yourself. Choose people you love, and upon whom you can depend. If your attendants are both men and women, call them "the People of Honor." If you don't want to designate any one person "above" another, you can make up specific titles: "Mensch of Honor," "Diva of Honor," and so forth. Or consider not having an honor attendant at all.

Concerned about leaving someone out? You can ask friends and family who are not in the wedding party to do a reading, sign the marriage license, give a toast, or help with another part of the ceremony or reception.

# All You Need Is **Love**

It's your wedding and you want to invite the world! Some guests are obvious—close family members and good friends. But what about your neighbors, your coworkers, and (yes, one bride actually did this) the mailman?

Keeping the guest list to those people who are genuinely important to you and your partner will help keep things simple, less expensive, and more personal.

*Here's a quick litmus test to use when trimming the guest list: Calculate the cost per head for your wedding. Then go through every name on the guest list with your partner. Would you take this person out for a restaurant meal worth that amount? If you respond with a resounding YES!, then invite that person. If you hesitate, give it some thought.*

## Earth-Friendly *Invitations*

For your wedding invitations and thank-you notes, consider using environment-friendly paper, which can be
gorgeous and indistinguishable from "regular" paper.

There are many different kinds of ecological paper, none
of which contains new wood fiber. Using ecological papers
reduces the demand for logging remaining forests, saves
water and energy in production, and doesn't add to our
landfills or pollute the water.

Also ask yourself: Do you really need an interior enve-
lope, tissue paper, and all those little cards? Keep your
invitations simple.

> **Speak to the earth, and it shall teach thee.**
>
> **—Old Testament**

I adore simple pleasures. They are the last refuge of the complex.

—Oscar Wilde

## Flower **Power**

Decorating with fresh flowers is an ancient and beautiful wedding tradition. Not only are the flowers gorgeous but they also smell divine. Using local, in-season blooms—as opposed to exotic, imported flowers—is a way of staying connected with the natural world (as well as keeping things simple and saving money).

Let Mother Nature be your guide: check out garden books or browse farmers' markets to find out what flowers are available in your part of the world during your wedding month. Depending on where you live, pink peonies may be at their peak in June, autumn leaves perfect in October, and holly and evergreen festive in December.

## Present *Laughter*

Registering for wedding gifts can be a great exercise in practicing nonattachment. You are inviting people to your wedding without the expectation of getting a gift in return, yes? And—of course—you'll love whatever it is people get you. Even the gold-plated wrench set.

But gift debacles can happen. Thirty guests may give you the same, off-the-registry-list gift item (blenders, anyone?). Some guests will simply forget about the gift. And some may express their ambivalence by forgetting "accidentally on purpose."

If you have no expectations to start with, and if you aren't attached to the idea of the gift registry, each present you do receive will be a true delight.

chapter 4

changing

relationships

Getting married marks a big change in people's lives. Even if you and your true love are already living together, your wedding marks the beginning of a new phase, and the people around you will be affected. You and your intended are entering a new, and more public, phase of your relationship. Other people may respond to your engagement with an unexpected reaction: your best friend elopes, your mom becomes an overprotective lioness, your in-laws-to-be become self-appointed wedding critics. Like birthdays with years ending in zero, weddings can bring up a lot of issues for people. Issues that have *nothing to do with you*. Remember that.

You may feel hurt when people around you say they're happy for you and yet act in a way that shows their ambivalence or self-absorption. It can throw you when your maid of honor "forgets" your shower, guests cancel at the last minute, or your sister gets a blue Mohawk (that clashes with her bridesmaid dress) two days before your wedding.

Of course, we want all the people around us to be overjoyed at the news of our nuptials—and most of them probably are. But when dealing with those who aren't, it helps not to be too attached to their reaction. Remember that want, *dukkha,* isn't always just about materialism. Want can be about expecting and needing particular responses from people and then being unhappy when we don't get them.

In this chapter, you'll learn how to avoid making assumptions or holding expectations about how people will behave. When you do have expectations (and you will—it's completely normal), try to recognize them and then let them go.

**Before trying to become a Buddha, first be kind to other people.**

**—*Chinese proverb***

## Making Your Partner **Your Priority**

It's ironic. Sometimes in the midst of a whirlwind of wedding planning, we find ourselves making time for everything—except our relationship with our partner. As exciting as it is to plan a wedding, it's important to keep the emphasis on your union, not just the day.

Take some time to be with your beloved. Take a walk, go out to dinner, fly a kite—do anything except talk about the *W* word. That's right—take a night off from discussing the Upcoming Event. You'll remember why you've decided to share your lives with each other— you're in love! Rejoice in that every day.

**And when Love speaks, the voice of all the gods
Makes heaven drowsy with the harmony.**

**—*William Shakespeare***

# To-may-to, **To-mah-to:**
## The Gentle Art of Compromise

A barefoot wedding at the beach versus a sophisticated gathering in a chic urban loft. A square-dancing hoedown in the backyard versus a grand affair in a hotel ballroom. It's all well and good for you to know what kind of wedding *you* really want—only to find your sweetie has a completely different idea in mind.

**I bend but do not break.**

**—Jean de La Fontaine**

Remember the Buddha's Middle Way—moderation in all things. Surely there's room for you both to compromise, merging both of your ideas about the kind of wedding you want to have. The result will be a unique, personal celebration. (And compromising is good practice for marriage.)

## You Did **What?**

"I asked my fiancé to go to the train station and pick up some of our friends and relatives. Well, he did, but he was hours late," says Jana. "We don't fight that much, but we really had a go-around that night. Even though I know Phil is the most trustworthy and reliable man on the planet, all I could think of was, 'What if this is how our marriage is going to be?'"

What Jana was doing was projecting her fears for the marriage onto a one-time action of Phil's (who, by the way, had gotten stuck in traffic). She wasn't dealing with the specific problem in the specific moment, but was instead projecting a lifetime of tardiness and forgetfulness. See why it's good to stay in the moment?

More than ten years later Jana is still happily married and reports, "Of course, that wasn't the case!"

## Care and Feeding of **Bridesmaids**

Your friends will be taking their cues from you. Treat them with respect, kindness, and compassion (and don't expect them to wear scary-looking, *très cher* dresses), and the rest will fall into place.

Yes, you're the bride, but remember—everyone's the star of his or her own life, including the people in your wedding party. And although you may be immersed in wedding-planning details, remember to be a friend. Check in with your friends and family about their lives, and schedule some time to hang out so you can listen and support what's going on with them.

*In France, it's the custom for the bride to let the bridesmaids pick out their own dresses. Ooh la la!*

## Control Freaks **Anonymous**

But *you're* not a control freak, right? There's a reason you love your friends—these people are so unique, so special, that the mold just had to be broken. You love them just as they are, so would you really want to try to make them do or say anything that's out of character, even for your wedding?

So what if Uncle Bernie wants to wear his favorite lime-green slacks, you loathe your maid of honor's date, and your best buddy hates to conga? They're your friends and family, people you want in your life for a long, long time to come. A little kindness and compassion go a long way.

## Family **Feud**

Is someone in your life (perhaps someone holding the purse strings) issuing ultimatums about some aspect of your wedding?

If the demands are presented as nonnegotiable, you'll need to make your desires known clearly. If the person still makes no move toward a satisfactory compromise, examine your *dukkha*—are you attached to the idea of getting this person's approval? Are you attached to the idea of their money? Is the attachment compromising your integrity?

Remember: It's your wedding. You and your partner ultimately need to please yourselves, which may mean setting limits (compassionately, but firmly) on other people's involvement in the planning. You may even need to give the money back.

**Most of the luxuries and many of the so-called comforts of life are not only not indispensable, but positive hindrances to the elevation of mankind.**

**—Henry David Thoreau**

## Dealing with **Divorced Parents**

Weddings often bring up issues for people, especially divorced parents. From paying for the wedding to deciding where they'll sit, to bringing dates and new partners—they can make you crazy if you're too attached to how they "should" behave. Remember, you can't control them. Ever.

What your parents, or your partner's parents, need to remember is that it's *your* wedding. It's not about them (even though they may see it that way). It's about the two of you. They need to put aside their differences (or at least keep them private) in order to make your day as stress-free as possible. And, happily, many will.

## **Problem** Parents

What if one of your parents (or a bridesmaid, or anyone, for that matter) tries to use your wedding as an excuse to act out?

Speak to the person, with your partner at your side if you want moral support. Tell her you love her and that you want her to be part of your wedding day. Be clear about your expectations, using "I" statements. Let the person share with you what's on her mind. With good communication, you'll be able to iron out most tense situations.

It's important to realize that it's the other person's problem—not yours. Not attaching to the problem makes not taking the argument personally that much easier.

"I" STATEMENTS *(for example, "I would appreciate it if you would be polite to Dad's new girlfriend") are a way to convey your message without alienating your listener. "I" statements put the responsibility on the speaker, unlike "You" statements ("Your senseless bickering is ruining my wedding!"), which put the listener on the defensive.*

NONATTACHMENT *is not assuming things will happen in a certain way and not taking things for granted. By practicing nonattachment (which is different from detachment, or apathy), we open ourselves up to different possibilities. We may not like these possibilities, but we can more easily accept them.*

## Trouble in *Nirvana*

It's hard when other people don't accept your beloved. After all, this is the person with whom you want to spend the rest of your life. Why can't they see how wonderful he or she is?

As an adult, you can't attach to the idea of family approval and still live your own life. You've chosen a wonderful person; as long as you're content with your decision, that's all you need. Of course, you could play the martyr, but the drama and pathos would drain your emotional stability and physical energy. The bottom line: When in doubt, your life and happiness—including your new life with your partner—come first.

But what if the shoe's on the other foot—your partner's family doesn't care for you? (Are they *insane?*) Instead of reaching for the boxing gloves, try compassion—the attachment-free variety.

In *The Art of Happiness,* His Holiness The Dalai Lama explains his philosophy of compassion: "One kind of compassion is tinged with attachment—the feeling of controlling someone, or loving someone so that person will love you back. . . . But there is a second type of compassion that is free from such attachment. . . . It is based on the other's fundamental rights rather than your own mental projection. Upon this basis, then, you will generate love and compassion. That's genuine compassion."

**I have noticed that folks are generally about as happy as they make up their minds to be.**

*—Abraham Lincoln*

# suddenly

*Where Wedding Fantasies End
and Real Life Begins*

While the bridal-magazine version of a wedding is a white-tulle-swathed fantasyland, a real wedding has a lot of, well, reality. Sometimes things happen that can, if we let them, make us a little crazy.

*Samsara* is a Sanskrit word for everyday life. While it's great to meditate and get to know yourself, the place that Zen living can really help you is the practical arena, where unexpected events test your patience, compassion, and ability to be present.

Plan your wedding without attachments, without excessive worry or need for ironclad control. Take care of yourself, physically and emotionally, so that you have the strength to deal with the trials and tribulations that will inevitably arise. Devote yourself to coping with unexpected challenges using compassion and grace.

In this chapter you'll learn techniques for dealing with all sorts of problems that never happened in *Father of the Bride:* how to manage "disaster," how to navigate complicated family decisions, and what to do when running off to Las Vegas starts to look good.

SAMSARA *is everyday life in the phenomenal world (the one in the here and now that we experience with our five senses). It can also refer to the cycle of life, death, and rebirth that Buddhists believe they experience before attaining nirvana.*

## "Disaster" and the **Zen Perspective**

When a couple is planning their wedding, unexpected things may happen. The dress order gets lost, the officiant has a nervous breakdown, or the caterers go out of business. To paraphrase a popular expression, stuff happens.

Of course, you'll have feelings about these things—who wouldn't? To deal with these unexpected occurrences, sit down and really feel the feelings they bring up. Then decide to let them go.

Remember that just as labeling an event a "disaster" will surely make it one, labeling the experience as just that— an experience—neutralizes it. You've then opened yourself to a whole new set of possibilities.

Something you had planned for your wedding didn't work. So what? Something else will. The real disaster would be if you let unforeseen glitches stand in the way of your enjoying your wedding.

**There is nothing either good or bad, but thinking makes it so.**

**—William Shakespeare**

# My *Two Dads*

Life is so much easier in the movies. When there's a wedding in a classic film there's not even a question that the bride will walk down the aisle with her father.

Real life is a little more complicated. Just in the father category alone, there are biological fathers, stepfathers, adoptive fathers, and godfathers. If you have both a biological father and a stepfather in your life, whom do you choose? Both? Neither? Are you even comfortable with the concept of being "given away"? If so, whom do you really want to do the giving?

As with so many of the personal decisions involved in wedding planning, it's best to please yourself, taking care to communicate your decision to others truthfully and thoughtfully. Have your mom and your dad walk you down the aisle, stride by yourself, or go hand in hand with your friends. One couple even waltzed themselves down the aisle. Whatever you choose, approach the place where you'll take your vows with confidence and grace.

## Viva **Las Vegas?**

"What was I *thinking?*"

Good question.

What happens when you feel you might lose it—and eloping to Las Vegas sounds like a good option? It's happened to almost everyone who's gone through the process of planning a wedding; at some point or another, the stress becomes overwhelming.

If you're that close to the end of your rope, you need to start taking better care of yourself. Have you been eating right, sleeping enough, taking time out to be alone? Is there something specific that's bothering you, something you need to address?

Maybe you really do want to chuck it all and elope, or maybe not. But you'll never know unless you spend some time by yourself. Eat a healthy dinner. Get a good night's sleep. Go back to meditating, breathing, and taking time to hang solo, away from the madding crowd.

Then make your decision.

**Take rest; a field that is rested gives a bountiful crop.**

**—Ovid**

## Keeping the *Faith*

Combining the traditions of two religions can be both exciting and intimidating. Interfaith couples must decide for themselves what aspects of each religious tradition they want to include in order to fashion a ceremony (or ceremonies) and reception with which they can both be comfortable.

Meditation and taking some reflective time alone will help you understand what's truly important to you, so that you can work with your partner (and your officiants) to plan a ceremony that reflects both your beliefs. Learn as much as you can about the religion or culture of your partner, as you explain and share your own beliefs and customs. It will help you understand your partner and your in-laws better, and they will understand you better as well.

## The *Bridal Bunch*

If you and/or your partner have children from a previous relationship, the kids will need to feel included in the wedding. After all, you're not just getting married—you're creating a new family. Kids may have concerns about what your new marriage will mean for them; it's important to let them know—often—that you love them more than ever.

Giving your and your partner's kids meaningful roles in your wedding will help reassure them of their continued importance in your life. Some couples even include a special ceremony for the children that focuses on the familial nature of marriage.

chapter

and beyond

So many people rush through their wedding day, fueled by adrenaline and low on blood sugar. Their day becomes a blur of tasks to be done: "Now I need to get dressed, now I need to get to the church, now we need to have our pictures taken—do I have lipstick on my teeth? Hurry— we're late!" They rush from wedding ceremony to receiving line to dinner to first dance and, before they know it, the day they've waited so long to experience is over.

Your commitment to being aware and present will help you savor your wedding day. You'll slow down, delighting in making your vows with your partner, enjoying the little moments, and connecting with people. You'll experience the day with all of your five senses— the feel of your dress as you slip it on, the smell of the lilies in your hair, the sight of your partner smiling as he or she sees you, the sound of the music, and the taste of wedding cake.

Take a deep breath, and approach the day with curiosity and an open heart. And have fun!

# My *One and Only*

On your wedding day there'll likely be such a flurry of excitement and so many people who want your attention that you may forget exactly why it is you're there— your partner.

In the Jewish faith it's traditional for the bride and groom to take a moment to be alone together, after the ceremony. If you choose to adopt this custom, you'll have some private time to catch your breath and connect with each other before rejoining the group.

Some couples decide to stay together during the entire reception. That way, not only do they have each other's support but they also have similar experiences and memories of the same events years later.

*Down the Aisle **in Style:***

*Calming the Wedding Day Jitters*

Use the day before and the morning of your wedding to really pamper yourself. This is a time not only to have a manicure or pedicure, but also to reflect on the meaning of the day and compose yourself for what's to come.

Here are some ideas:

- Consider getting a massage, which will help you relax physically and mentally.

- Get enough sleep—no all-hours partying the night before!

- Breathe.

- Take time out in the morning to be alone—write in your journal, take a bath, contemplate your morning coffee.

- Breathe.

- On the day of the wedding, do not—repeat—do *not* forget to eat breakfast! (Fainting as you walk down the aisle is not optimal.)

- Breathe.

- Have fun!

- *Breathe.* (When people are excited, sometimes they can breathe erratically or take shallow breaths, depriving the brain of oxygen. If you need to, have someone in your wedding party remind you to breathe deeply at regular intervals during the day.)

## *Stop and Smell* **the Bridal Bouquet**

By now you know how important it is to stay in the present moment. But on your wedding day, with all the accompanying adrenaline, excitement, and nervousness, it's more of a challenge.

To focus yourself, take a moment to look—really look—at your bouquet. Look at the colors of the flowers, feel the textures of the blooms, smell the fragrance. Really experience what it's like to be in the present moment.

During the day, when you look down at your bouquet, you'll remember to concentrate on being in the present moment.

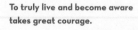

**To truly live and become aware takes great courage.**

**—*Gourasana***

## *Kicking Up Your* **Ruby Slippers**

Living in the moment is challenging at the best of times, but it's downright impossible if your feet hurt.

Have you ever found yourself perched on teeny-tiny high heels, smiling through your pain? Take that feeling and multiply it by a hundred for your wedding day, because you will rarely—if ever—sit down. You will be walking, you will be talking, you will be dancing, but you will definitely *not* be sitting.

One particular bride wore, under her very traditional white gown, red patent-leather penny loafers and white bobby socks. No one realized what she was wearing on her feet until the reception, when she and the groom started dancing and her skirts swirled. One of the most touching photos was a close-up of the bride's and groom's feet during the first dance.

**Present mirth hath present laughter.**

**—William Shakespeare**

## Be Our *Guest*

Your family and friends have dropped everything, some possibly traveling long distances at great personal expense, to come to your wedding and celebrate with you. As a couple, take the time to speak with everyone at your wedding, to greet them and thank them for coming.

Cherish the gathering. You'll most likely never have all of those particular people assembled again. Take a moment to appreciate it.

chapter 7

You Mean There's Life

*after*

the wedding?

Huzzah—you did it! You're married! Maybe you've even gone on and returned from the honeymoon trip. You're probably now starting to see other people's photographs of your wedding and opening lots of presents, as well as being called (wink wink, nudge nudge) "the newlyweds."

Maybe you're making a smooth transition to married life. But part of you (even just a *little* part) might feel sad that all the excitement is over—that's normal. You put a lot of time, emotional energy, and money into your wedding. It was a big deal.

But so is real life. Remember—Zen is all about living in the now. What's your now looking like? With the transition to this new stage, it's even more important to stay in the present and keep in touch with the real you.

 **How much the wife is dearer than the bride.**

*—Lord Lyttleton*

## Gratitude *Attitude*

The idea of gratitude is a very Zen one: gratitude for the present moment, for everyday wonders, for the gift of life, for breath itself.

As you open the gifts people have given you and your sweetie, it's important to express your gratitude. Promptly send the giver a meaningful thank-you note—not just for the gift but also for his or her good wishes, presence, and support on your wedding day.

## Couple **Karma**

*Karma,* in the Zen sense, is a somewhat misunderstood term. It's not actually a system of reward (or punishment) but instead a philosophy of cause and effect: if you put energy out, at some point in time it will flow back to you.

Another way to show gratitude, in a more general sense, is for you and your partner to make a charitable contribution as a couple. Getting married is a wonderful opportunity to discover and define what causes and organizations you both deem worth supporting.

KARMA *is the Sanskrit word for the universal law of cause and effect.*

## Marriage **Zen**

Like weddings, marriage can sometimes be challenging—
but the rewards are infinite. And, just as in wedding
planning, it's important for you to live in the present.
Stay in touch with the real you. Practice nonattachment. Take the Middle Way. Find joy in everyday living.
And keep a sense of humor.

Have a wonderful life!

**Life's like a movie. Write your own ending.**

—*The Muppet Movie*

# acknowledgments

A deep bow of appreciation to Idria Barone Knecht, for her advice and encouragement.

Namaste to Ji Hyang Sunim, for her advice and insight into the philosophy of Zen.

A shower of lotus petals for the following: Stephanie D'Abruzzo and Craig Shemin, Fidelma Fitzpatrick and Jim Rooney, Amy Kass and Jonathan Amsterdam, Mary Max and Peter Max, Emily Prenner and Chris Steele, Jana Riess and Phil Smith, Elizabeth Riley and Darren Johnson, Lisa Rogers and James Byrne.

A special thank you to Robert and Shirley Elia, and Edna MacNeal, all of whom could not have been more supportive and helpful during our wedding.

Nosegays of daffodils to Mieck Coccia and Arielle Eckstut of Levine Greenberg Communications, and bouquets of pink roses to Mikyla Bruder and Lisa Campbell of Chronicle Books.